Dog
Alert

ALISON LOHANS

Published by Pearson Education Limited, Edinburgh Gate, Harlow, Essex, CM20 2JE
Registered company number: 872828

www.pearsonschools.co.uk

First published by Pearson
a division of Pearson New Zealand Ltd
67 Apollo Drive, Rosedale, North Shore 0632, New Zealand
Associated companies throughout the world

Text © Pearson 2011

Page Layout, Design and Illustrations: Mark Glover

The right of Alison Lohans to be identified as author of this work has been asserted
by her in accordance with the Copyright, Designs and Patents Act 1988.

First published 2011
This edition published 2012

2024
12

British Library Cataloguing in Publication Data
A catalogue record for this book is available from the British Library

ISBN 978-0-43507-591-0

Printed in Great Britain by Ashford Colour Press Ltd.

Acknowledgements
We would like to thank the children and teachers of Bangor Central Integrated
Primary School, NI; Bishop Henderson C of E Primary School, Somerset; Brookside
Community Primary School, Somerset; Cheddington Combined School,
Buckinghamshire; Cofton Primary School, Birmingham; Dair House Independent
School, Buckinghamshire; Deal Parochial School, Kent; Lawthorn Primary School,
North Ayrshire; Newbold Riverside Primary School, Rugby and Windmill Primary
School, Oxford for their invaluable help in the development and trialling of the Bug
Club resources.

Every effort has been made to contact copyright holders of material reproduced in
this book. Any omissions will be rectified in subsequent printings if notice is given
to the publishers.

A division of Pearson New Zealand Ltd

Contents

Chapter 1

Uranium Point

The propellers had been droning for a couple of hours and their sound filled the tiny plane. Bracing herself, Zoe looked out the window. The vast white, blackish-green and grey Canadian north swooped closer as they descended. All that snow! For as far as the eye could see, forests of jack pine and spruce lay in dark blankets over the white. Leafless birch trees reached upwards like bony skeletons.

"We're going to live *here*?" Zoe's brother, Bailey, moaned from across the aisle.

Dad laughed. "It's our adventure," he said.

"Not *too* much of one, I hope!" Mum said.

Zoe shivered. Until now, this trip to Canada had seemed so exciting. Dad and Mum would be working at the North Star Inn for the next few months. Dad's friend Colin had bought the business, moved to Canada, then hired them to renovate it. But it was so far from home! Maybe this was what people meant when they talked about having cold feet – though her feet didn't feel anything at all.

Dog Alert

In the little cockpit, one of the pilots was looking at a map while the other worked the controls. Both of them wore headphones. Zoe wondered if they were as cold as she felt. The whole family was bundled in winter gear – and they needed it. A lot of their luggage was strapped into the back of the plane, but some things had been stashed in the nose. Would her clothes freeze up there?

The great white stretch beneath them was a lake. Just as Zoe spotted a winding trail of dark ice near the shore, one of the pilots turned around. "There's the ice road!" she shouted over the noise of the plane.

Immediately, Dad started going on about how transport trucks travelled those roads to remote places – and how, when the ice melted, the road would be gone. The only way to get in or out of Uranium Point would be by plane. When Dad got excited, he was a walking encyclopedia.

Off to the west, Zoe could see a long blue crack stretching across the ice. She pointed it out to Bailey, who just shrugged. Zoe tried not to think of Hannah – she was probably lying in the sun on the beach at home right now. And Gram, who'd been dead set against their trip from the start.

The little plane banked, turning away from the white lake. Now Zoe could see a few small buildings scattered about. Nearby, a grey strip sprawled across the snow. "That's it!" she cried.

"It's *tiny*!" Disappointment echoed in Bailey's voice.

Zoe wondered what living in such a remote place would be like. Although it was March and the Canadian calendar said it was spring, this was definitely still winter.

The plane circled and dipped towards the settlement and, before long, they'd landed. Trees and small buildings raced by as the plane shuddered to a stop.

Dog Alert

The pilots stood up. "Welcome to Uranium Point!" one of them said.

Zoe waited while everyone went to the back of the plane. She could hear thumps as bags and boxes were unloaded and people went up and down the skinny steps leading to the ground.

Finally, Dad was back. "Ready, Zo?" he asked with a grin, and scooped her up. She clung to him as they lurched down the steps. Her wheelchair waited forlornly on the snowy tarmac. An orange windsock fluttered and the air smelled fresh and clean.

Gram's fierce whispers echoed in Zoe's mind. "You've got no business taking that poor child to the wilderness. At the other end of the world, no less!" Gram had thought Zoe wasn't listening – but she'd been wrong. For the first time, Zoe wondered if maybe Gram had been right.

Mum had quickly retorted, "Zoe's a brave girl. You don't realise how much she can do."

At the time, she'd wanted to hug Mum for sticking up for her.

Now, the cold wrapped around her. Her wheelchair felt like an ice cube. When Dad set her down, the cold from the armrests reached right through her jacket sleeves. Good thing she was wearing her mittens. She buckled her seatbelt and released the brakes. Grasping the wheel rims, she pushed herself forward. It was hard work. The wheels crunched in the snow.

As the others began carrying the luggage to the small airport building, Zoe did her best to keep up. It wasn't easy.

A sign posted on the wall of the building read: WARNING: DO NOT WALK ALONE AT NIGHT. DOG PACKS CAN BE DANGEROUS.

Were these dogs *wild*? Zoe glanced at Bailey, who caught her eye.

"Just what you always wanted," he teased. "A whole pack of dogs."

"As if," she retorted. She couldn't let on how nervous she felt or Bailey would tease her mercilessly. Ever since a big dog had jumped up on her and nipped her chin when she was small, she'd been scared of them. Dogs got nervous around *her,* too. Some acted like her chair was an alien creature, snapping and growling at it.

Zoe pushed away the scary thoughts. At least she'd have lots of things to tell Hannah and the kids at school about Uranium Point. "Race you inside!" she said.

"Yeah, right." Bailey gave her a scornful look, but took off running anyway. He won, of course.

Chapter 2
North Star Inn

Dad's friend Colin led them out to an old van. Zoe felt like one of the bags when Dad put her into the van first, along with her chair. People kept cramming things in until the van was packed as full as a tin of sardines. Zoe couldn't stop shivering.

Mum scooted in beside her. "Zoe, you're cold!" she said.

"It's okay," she said through chattering teeth. With Mum and Bailey squished in beside her, it was warmer already. In the front, Dad and Colin were talking nonstop.

The van jostled over bumpy, hilly roads. Zoe stared out at small houses, fuel tanks, a tiny gas station and trees. They went past the school. It was much smaller than the one at home. Would the kids like her? She might have trouble fitting in at first.

"Here we are," Colin said, turning up a steep hill.

NORTH STAR INN read a faded, peeling sign.

The building desperately needed a coat of paint. Old trucks sat by the entrance. Low wooden steps led to the front door.

Zoe's stomach sank. They were going to live *here*? And a large dog was wandering about. "Colin," Zoe said, "is that your dog?"

Colin didn't hear – Dad was talking to him.

Mum patted her arm. "He looks like a friendly dog, doesn't he?"

Bailey jostled her other arm, pointing to the snowy front steps. "Have fun getting in, sis," he said.

Zoe bristled. "Dad'll build me a ramp," she said.

While the others began unpacking, she longed for home – for the sloping ramp that led to the house, for their comfortable van with its wheelchair lift. When she and Hannah went places, she used her sliding board to transfer between the car and her chair. But this van was so large, her board was useless.

Zoe shook herself. The car accident that had left her paralysed was long ago. Getting around in her chair was simply how things were. At home, everything was normal – but here, it wasn't. *Not yet*, she reminded herself.

"Dad!" she shouted as he walked by, whistling. "Are you going to leave me sitting here forever?"

"Oops, sorry, Zo." Dad got her wheelchair out and unfolded it. "Don't want to keep my best girl waiting."

"Dad?" she said as he lifted her. "Is everything going to be weird here?"

For a moment his eyes met hers. "Are you worried, Zoe?" he asked.

"Yeah," she admitted. "What about that dog?" The large animal was still nosing around. "Is it part wolf? Will it get upset by my chair?"

Dad set her down. He paused before answering. "He's a husky. A sled dog, Colin says. Apparently he belonged to some old guy who died, and now he hangs around getting food from anyone who'll feed him. Don't worry, Colin says he hasn't gone wild, like some of the others."

Dad pulled an armful of bags out of the van and put a small one in Zoe's lap. "Hey, Bailey!" he called as her brother strode past. "Go and help Mum unpack in the kitchen, *pronto*. She has to make dinner for a dozen construction workers and miners." He shook his head and walked off, muttering about unpleasant surprises.

Zoe sucked in a frustrated breath. Dad was being his usual preoccupied self. Everybody was busy. She'd get herself to the door, then she'd yell, call or something.

Dog Alert

She pulled her mobile out of her jacket pocket. Mum insisted she keep it with her at all times, for emergencies. She pressed the power switch. The display lit up, but the familiar logo didn't appear. NO SERVICE, the screen read.

"Hi!" a voice called.

Startled, Zoe looked up. Across the road, a boy about her age was staring at her.

"Hi," she replied. Would he come over to talk to her? Instead, the boy simply nodded, then ran away across a snowy yard. Zoe tucked her phone away and grasped her wheels. The snow crunched and squeaked as she rolled towards the entrance. Gravel showed through footprints in the snow. This was going to be harder than she'd expected.

Woof!

Zoe's heart jumped. She pushed herself forward as fast as she could. But the dog reached her. From her position in the wheelchair, its head was the same height as her own. Still barking, it blocked her way.

"Go away!" she shouted.

Instead, the dog moved in closer. Brown eyes stared right at her. They seemed to be smiling. Pointed ears stood upright. The dog's tan and black fur was fluffier than any teddy bear she'd ever seen.

A second dog appeared, a smaller, scruffy one. Its face seemed flattened and its eyes looked mean to Zoe.

"Mum!" Zoe yelled. "Dad!"

Nobody answered. Zoe looked at the entrance to the North Star Inn. Should she barge ahead?

The big dog sniffed at her motionless feet. Then it lifted its leg. It peed on one of the small front wheels of her chair.

Horrified, Zoe tried to roll forward. Her footrest struck the smaller dog.

It growled.

Zoe screamed.

Chapter 3

Too Close for Comfort!

The dogs pressed closer. The big one barked. Its warm breath brushed Zoe's face like a damp mist. The smaller dog growled again. Its pointy teeth looked sharp.

Fear prickled her neck. "Dad!" she screamed. "Help!"

To her relief, the door screeched open. "Hey!" Bailey ran towards her. The dogs raced over to him, barking.

The wheelchair jolted as her brother seized the handles. Grabbing the rims, Zoe helped push towards the building. Bailey grunted as he turned her chair around and hauled the large back wheels onto the first step. It was impossible to go further. Noisily, the dogs crowded in.

"Dad!" she yelled again. "*Help*!"

Colin appeared in the doorway. "Scram!" he roared. Surprisingly, the dogs slunk away.

Zoe sat there shaking as Colin hoisted her the rest of the way up. The wheelchair jammed in the narrow doorway. Stuck!

Zoe bit her lip to hold back tears.

Colin muttered something. He gave a great heave. With a splintering sound, part of the door frame broke off. He grinned at her: "Needed fixing anyhow."

"Zoe?" Mum hurried into the front lobby. "Are you all right?"

Zoe tried hard not to cry. It was freezing cold, that dog had peed on her wheelchair, and her chair had broken the door frame. She didn't fit here. Not at all.

"Zoe?" Mum said again, looking worried.

"It was dogs!" Excitedly, Bailey told his part of the story. Luckily, he hadn't seen the dog peeing, otherwise she'd never hear the end of it.

"Thank goodness nothing happened." Mum patted her shoulder. "Sorry, Zoe, but I have a huge dinner to cook." She disappeared through a doorway – one that wasn't scraped and broken.

"You okay, sis?" Bailey asked.

Zoe's teeth chattered. "Yeah, but I'm *cold.*"

"You should see the TV!" Bailey said. "We've got satellite! There's *hundreds* of channels. This is going to be so cool!"

"Bailey!" Dad called from somewhere. "I need your help. Then Mum needs you to peel potatoes."

Bailey rolled his eyes. "How come Zoe can't do that?" he shouted back.

"Bailey. Right now."

"Lucky you," he muttered. "Potatoes – ugh!"

Zoe assessed the heaps of luggage. A woolly red blanket stuck out from under a duffle bag. She wheeled over to get it. Like everything else, the blanket was cold, but she draped it around herself.

An old computer monitor sat on a desk in the lobby. Above it, a moose head stared down at her with glassy eyes. She heard things being dragged. Then she heard the banging of a hammer.

What was she supposed to do, just sit? "Dad?" she called. "What should I do?"

The banging stopped. "What was that you said, Zoe?"

Suddenly she was mad. "I said, *what should I do*?" she yelled again, louder.

"Uh . . ." There were two more bangs. "I know," Dad said. "My little brown tool chest. If you can bring it . . ." *Bang.*

Zoe wheeled across the ratty carpet. Floorboards squeaked. The blanket trailed behind her. She grabbed the handle of Dad's tool chest. "Got it," she called, starting down the hall.

The carpet was loose. Before she'd gone far, a large fold rolled up and stopped her. Gritting her teeth, Zoe pushed forwards. More carpet came away from the floor. Now it was caught on the frame of her chair.

Dad didn't seem to be waiting. He was talking to Bailey and the banging had resumed. Probably he didn't even need that tool chest.

The hallway was too narrow to turn around. Frustrated, Zoe backed into the lobby. Now the blanket caught in her wheels – and the moose head looked mad at her. Could she get down the other hall? No, too much stuff blocked her way.

It wasn't fair! Zoe stared out the front window. Except for those trucks, there wasn't much to see besides the house across the road and the snowy hillside. She set the tool chest on the floor and made a face at the moose head.

Supper was in a large room with several tables. Men sat eating hungrily. Mum looked really tired. Hot, too, despite the cold outside.

Bailey kept asking Colin about igloos. Colin laughed and shook his head, while Dad droned on about the renovations.

Zoe toyed with her potatoes. Everybody had stared when she came in. Her chair hadn't fitted through the doorway, so Dad carried her in, while Bailey collapsed the chair and brought it to a table. Was this how things would be from now on? Having to wait for people to help her. She wasn't going to like it.

While everybody else cleared up, she sat shuffling a deck of cards. Finally, Bailey appeared. "What a mess!" he said. "Mum's grouchy as anything. And Dad just dropped a stack of plates." He wandered over to a window and looked out into the darkness. "Guess I can't explore," he said wistfully. "Not with those dogs."

"Want to play?" Zoe asked desperately.

"May as well," Bailey said with a sigh, but before they'd even finished one game, he wandered off to watch TV.

All the travelling must've caught up with her. The next thing Zoe knew, Mum was helping her get ready for bed. She hardly remembered getting into her pyjamas or using her sliding board to transfer into bed.

However, once Mum left the room, she couldn't sleep. The bed jounced and creaked every time she moved. There was a lump she couldn't avoid. A limp curtain hung over the small window. If only she could reach her board and get back into her chair to look outside.

In the distance, dogs barked.

Would Uranium Point be more than she could handle? Maybe Gram was right.

Chapter 4
School

"I'll push myself!" Zoe whispered sharply to Mum as they left the school office. Her stomach twisted. She could hear her wheels rasping on the carpet as the secretary led the way. Bailey had to leave his boots at the front door, so he was walking around in his socks.

She knew everybody would stare. Once again she wished they were home, where everyone was used to her.

The red and white Canadian flag hung in the entrance with its big red maple leaf in the middle. The Queen's portrait was on a wall nearby. For some reason, Zoe thought of the moose head at the North Star Inn. It was like the boss of the lobby. She steered herself around a corner. Cheerful classroom noises greeted them.

The noise stopped when they entered. Luckily, Bailey went in first and thank goodness Mum didn't follow. Zoe's hands were sweaty as she navigated her way through the doorway. Everyone's eyes were on her.

Quickly, she glanced around. It was a small class and the kids were different ages. She recognised the boy from yesterday. He smiled faintly. Zoe smiled back, then looked away. She didn't want to stare.

The teacher, Mrs Piper, was friendly. "Welcome to the north, Zoe and Bailey," she said, extending her hand. She sounded foreign, just like everyone else here.

Zoe leaned forward to shake hands with Mrs Piper. "Thank you," she said, realising her own accent was the one that was foreign here in Canada.

Bailey spoke up. "Is it always this cold?" he asked.

The kids laughed and gave a chorus of answers. Relieved, Zoe waited while Mrs Piper seated Bailey at a desk. Then she indicated a table at the side of the room. "Will this be all right, Zoe?" she asked. "Can you see the board?"

"Yes, thanks." As Zoe rolled to the table she could feel everybody staring.

Mrs Piper asked them about home and their trip to Uranium Point. Some of the kids couldn't stop looking at the wheelchair. "Can you walk?" a boy asked curiously.

Zoe shook her head. "My legs are paralysed," she said. "From a car accident. I sort of remember walking, when I was little."

The classroom went silent.

Bailey caught her eye. "Zoe can do lots of things," he said. Would he mention how good she was at basketball? Or that, when they'd done archery, she'd got several bull's-eyes?

No such luck. Instead, Bailey asked if there was a soccer team. The kids all started talking about skiing and sliding and ice fishing.

At last, Mrs Piper began a spelling lesson. Jetlag caught up with Zoe again. It was suddenly hard to keep her eyes open.

A loud bell jolted her awake. Immediately, kids were on their feet, shrugging into jackets. Zoe looked longingly at her brother, who was clustered among the boys.

"Bailey," one of them said, "come and slide with us. You can use my saucer."

Mrs Piper smiled at Zoe and turned to the girls. "Leah, why don't you show Zoe around at morning break."

As Bailey followed the boys out, three girls hurried over. They were all talking at once, so Zoe couldn't figure out which one was Leah. "Want me to push you?" one of the girls offered.

Most people couldn't handle a chair. They bumped things or went too fast. "I can do it," she said. "Thanks," she added, at the girl's disappointed look.

"Is this yours?" Another girl held out Zoe's pink jacket. "Will you be warm enough?"

Zoe let the girls help her into her jacket and then rolled along beside them. Outside, wind gusted into her face. At the end of the playground, Bailey was towing a bright red plastic circle up a hill. He was laughing.

"Do you want to slide?" a girl in a yellow jacket asked hesitantly. She'd just picked up a purple plastic disc.

Couldn't they tell she had no way of getting over there? "Uh . . ."

"Eva!" another girl said, shocked. "Can't you see that she . . ."

The girl's face turned pink. "Oh, sorry," she mumbled.

A dog bounded over to them. Wagging its tail, it pushed against the girl called Eva.

Eva laughed and petted the dog. "I love you, too, Sparkles. But you should go home. You know dogs aren't allowed on the playground." The other girls gathered around, petting the dog.

Zoe realised she was holding her breath.

The dog was so *big*!

"Want to pat Sparkles, Zoe?" Eva grasped the dog's fur and led it closer, even as Zoe shrank back in her chair. The dog gave a soft *Wuff*! and cautiously approached. It sniffed the wheel where the other dog had peed.

"No!" Zoe gasped. One of the girls gave Zoe a startled look. "Don't you like dogs?" she asked.

Zoe didn't know what to say. "The airport has a sign about dog packs . . ."

All three girls started talking at once about wild dogs, mean ones, dogs that got run over chasing trucks. Before Zoe had a chance to ask the important question – would she be safe in her wheelchair? – the girls wandered

off towards the hill with Sparkles wagging his tail beside them. Then they were running and sliding with the boys.

Loneliness wrapped its arms around Zoe. Here she was out in the snow – abandoned and shivering. Why had they ever come to Uranium Point?

Then she tensed. Something was coming up behind her. Two large snowy paws plopped onto her lap. A dog's grinning face pushed towards hers. Was it the same dog as yesterday?

Zoe screamed.

The dog looked uncertain, but stayed where it was. It had warm, smelly breath.

"Go away!" Zoe shouted at it. Should she push it? The dog didn't look like it would bite, but how could she tell? She couldn't help it – another scream burst out.

Where was Bailey? On the hill, kids were staring and pointing. A couple of them ran towards her – but Bailey just stood there.

The principal appeared. "Nikita!" he yelled. "Down!" He gave the dog a shove. The dog obediently trotted away.

Dog Alert

Some of the kids gathered around. Despite the freezing cold, Zoe's face flamed. What could she say? Nearby, a couple of boys were snickering. One of them was Bailey.

How could he? Zoe clenched her teeth.

The bell rang.

The rest of the day was awkward. At gym time, kids were disappointed that they couldn't go skiing. Zoe knew it was because of her. Instead, they raced back and forth across the gym.

The only time she felt really good was in art. Their assignment was to draw animals. Studying a picture of a deer, she relaxed and began sketching it. She loved drawing. As the animal took shape on the page, Zoe noticed somebody looking over her shoulder.

It was the boy who'd said hi the day before. "That's really good," he said.

"Thanks," she said shyly.

He smiled. "I'm Eldon." He stepped away, but a minute later he was back with his pencil and paper. His drawing was of a large bird. It was so realistic Zoe almost expected it to move. Its eye stared right at her.

"That's awesome!" she said. "What kind of bird is it?"

"A raven," he said. "Don't you have those at home?"

"No." Zoe shook her head. Eldon pulled out a chair and sat down, but she couldn't think of anything else to say. They sat there, happily drawing.

When the bell rang, Bailey and one of the boys were talking excitedly about something called skidooing.

Zoe glared at her brother. How could he *laugh* at her? Especially in front of all the kids! Mum and Dad would get on his case for sure, if she told them. And, whatever skidooing was, she was sure she couldn't do it.

Dog Alert

Chapter 5

Dog Sled Ride

Mum and Dad were busy all the time. Right away they built a ramp so Zoe could get herself in and out of the North Star Inn. They widened all the doorways and got rid of the old carpet. Everything was dusty and the air smelled like carpet glue – but Zoe could finally get around.

Bailey went skidooing with Tyson one day. Afterwards, he couldn't stop talking about it. "It was awesome!" he said again after supper. His face shone. "We went so fast! We were on Killer Hill – you know, part of that steep hill outside? Tyson let me drive! I hit a bump and we were airborne!"

Zoe tuned out. Nobody had invited *her* to do anything. On TV, a commercial showed a car muffler repair place. She wished she could put a muffler on Bailey. Hannah hadn't emailed. There was nobody to talk to except her brother – and he only wanted to hang out with Tyson.

Should she phone one of the girls? They always talked about TV, and sliding and skiing and building snow forts – just like the boys. With the renovations at the North Star Inn, she couldn't invite someone over. And, if she did, who would it be? Eva maybe?

Mum hurried by, looking stressed.

"Mum?" she said. "Can I . . ." But Mum disappeared down the hall. Miners who lived at the inn walked by, talking about a hockey game. The whine of a saw cut through Bailey's excited chatter. Then someone clapped her on the shoulder. She looked up, startled.

"Don't know what to do?" Colin grinned down at her. He shooed Bailey away, saying, "Your dad needs a hand."

Ashamed, Zoe shook her head. "Everyone's busy. I'm just in the way and . . ." Suddenly, she found herself telling Colin all kinds of things. *Except* about how Bailey was treating her at school and how the dogs scared her.

As usual, the stray had been wandering around when Mum brought her back to the inn after school.

Colin's brow furrowed. The telephone rang in the lobby. He went to answer it.

Zoe fiercely blinked away tears. Her hand balled into a fist. She squeezed so hard it hurt. She pounded the armrest. When she pounded it again, her hand bounced off and hit her leg. She watched her knee jiggle. Why couldn't she *do* anything?

Colin was back. "I just had an idea," he said. "I'll pay you if you can help out."

"*Pay* me? For a job?" Zoe sat straighter.

Colin nodded. "Those miners and construction workers get pretty dirty. There's tons of laundry. I wouldn't expect you to collect the sheets and towels. But, if you could do the wash and fold everything afterwards, it would be great."

"Sure!" A job! And she'd even get paid! Zoe wondered about folding the sheets though – were they too big to handle? Would Bailey help if she offered to pay him? "Should I start now?"

Colin smiled. "Eager, eh?"

The phone rang again. Colin answered it. "For you, Miss Zoe," he yelled.

Mystified, Zoe raced to the lobby as fast as she could. Who could be calling her? Colin handed her the phone. She held it to her cheek. "Hello?"

"Hey, Zoe." The boy's voice was familiar. "It's me, Eldon. My uncle's coming with his dog team. My grandpa wonders if you'd like a ride? We're going on Saturday."

A dog sled ride! *Could* she?

Colin was grinning. "I heard that," he said. "Go for it. You'll love it! Not many people get to go dog sledding."

Suddenly she was soaring with joy. "*Thanks*, Eldon!" The moose head on the wall stared at her. "Can my brother come, too?" she added reluctantly. Tempting as it was to do something special without him, it would be easier if Bailey came along. Then maybe he'd be nicer at school, too. Today, on the way out to lunch, Eva had giggled when Tyson made a joke about wheelchair basketball players he'd seen on TV – and Bailey hadn't said a thing.

On Saturday, Zoe and Bailey bundled up in their warmest clothes. Outside, the crisp, cold air tingled Zoe's cheeks. Her breath floated in clouds around her. Dog sledding! She could hardly believe it.

Eldon ran across the road to meet them. "My grandpa will be here any minute," he said.

Bailey couldn't keep still. "This is *so* cool!" he said over and over. "Thanks for inviting me, sis."

Eldon glanced at Zoe and grinned. Then a man drove up in an old truck. Eldon beckoned to them to follow. Zoe pushed herself forwards on the packed snow, refusing offers of help.

She liked Eldon's grandpa instantly. His eyes twinkled. "So you're the budding artist Eldon told me about," he said. "Welcome to the north." Zoe liked that he didn't say anything about her disability.

Getting into the truck was tricky, even with Eldon's grandpa and Bailey lifting her. Finally, Zoe was on the front seat. She grabbed the steering wheel and slid over to the middle. Once everyone was buckled in, the old man shifted gears and drove out of town. When they stopped at a cabin in the forest, Zoe heard the clamour of dogs barking. Her insides shivered.

Eldon's uncle noticed her anxious look as he helped her out of the truck and into her chair. "Are you scared of dogs?" he asked.

"A little," Zoe admitted.

He nodded. "Makes sense," he said. "But don't worry. These dogs are sweet-tempered. You should meet the leaders. They're the smartest of the lot."

Eldon's grandpa pushed her chair through the snow. The snow wasn't packed here, and the front wheels kept bogging down. "It's easier if you tip the wheels up," she said, instead of waiting for Bailey to explain. They stopped beside a sled and the line of barking dogs harnessed to it.

"They just love to run," said Eldon's uncle. "That's when they're happiest." He whistled and the two lead dogs trotted over in their long harness.

Dog Alert

With all the barking, Zoe couldn't hear their names. Cautiously, she extended her hand. Black noses sniffed at her. Intelligent brown eyes looked at her.

Bailey and Eldon crowded in beside her to meet the dogs, and Zoe sighed with relief.

Soon afterwards, she was on the sled with Bailey behind her and Eldon in front. Eldon's uncle stepped on the runners in the back and shouted a command to the dogs. Instantly, the barking stopped and the dogs leapt forward. As they ran, the sled swished across the snow and picked up speed. Zoe gripped the sides. Fresh air whooshed in her face. She laughed out loud. They were flying!

Trees swept by. The string of dogs raced up and down hills and around curves. Sometimes it seemed they'd crash for sure, but the shouts of Eldon's uncle guided them.

Zoe couldn't stop laughing. It was the happiest she'd felt in a long time. Behind her, Bailey was laughing, too.

Suddenly, one dog ran sideways around a rock. The sled hit a bump. For a scary instant, Zoe really was flying. Then she hit the snow hard, face first. Shouts and barking filled the air.

Zoe fought back tears and struggled to roll sideways. Her legs stayed where they were. She pushed up with her strong arms, trying not to let panic take over.

Her heart stopped in her chest as she found herself face to face with a barking dog. Zoe screamed.

Chapter 6
The Quarrel

Eldon's uncle hurried over to her. "Noodles!" he yelled. "It's okay, Zoe," he added. "She's only barking. She won't hurt you."

Zoe tried to calm down, but she felt so helpless. The dog thrust its nose into her face and sniffed. She fought the urge to scream again.

"Are you okay?" Eldon's uncle asked, kneeling down beside her.

"Yeah," she said. She wished she could sit up. The dog began licking her chin.

"Noodles!" he yelled again. "Back." The dog retreated obediently. "Sorry about that spill. Tonka gets too independent every now and then. Now, how do we get you up?"

"Um …" How to explain? Bailey was sitting on a log, rubbing his head. Eldon looked embarrassed, as if he didn't know what to do.

"If you lift me up, I'll grab on," Zoe said.

After he'd helped her back into the sled, Eldon's uncle looked at the trail ahead, then at Zoe. "I think we should call it a day," he said.

Zoe saw the disappointment flash across Eldon's face. Bailey rolled his eyes and kicked at the snow. White powder flew everywhere, coating Zoe's jacket and mittens.

Nobody said much as they circled back and the dogs pulled them through the forest to Eldon's grandpa's cabin. Zoe blinked through tears at the sight of her chair waiting in the snow, near the truck.

Why did she have to ruin everything!

"How was the dog sledding?" Mum asked excitedly when they returned to the inn.

"Great," said Bailey, "until *she* fell out and made a massive deal about it and we had to stop." He stormed into his room and slammed the door.

Zoe's cheeks burned red. More than ever before, she longed for home.

She went to the laundry room to distract herself with the work for Colin. An enormous mountain of sheets, pillowcases and towels hulked in one corner. She got to work. Soon, she was buried in laundry. Sheets draped over her as she bent to pick them up. They caught in her wheels as she took them to the washing machines. Before long, she was sweating. She gave the next sheet such a strong tug, it billowed up over her head.

There was a shout of laughter. She turned around.

"Zoe the zombie!" Bailey said, leaning against the door, his arms crossed.

Angrily, she pulled the sheet off herself. "How come you've been mean to me ever since we moved here?" she demanded. "How come you never stick up for me at school?"

Bailey looked uncomfortable. "Dunno."

"*You don't know*? I don't even have friends here, so how come you have to make it worse?" She flung the sheet at her brother.

Bailey caught it, of course. "What're you doing?" he asked.

"What does it look like? I'm working – and *I'm* getting paid." Zoe grabbed a towel and threw it, too.

"Paid?" he yelped. "I have to work for free."

"Serves you right," she said.

Bailey scowled. "Colin should've given the job to me. At least I'm not in a wheelchair!"

Something exploded inside her. She rammed her chair straight into her brother.

Bailey thudded against a washing machine. "Hey, Zoe!" he yelled. "What's the matter with you?"

"What's the matter with *me*?" she yelled back at him. "What's the matter with *you*?" Sobbing, she fled down the hall to her room.

Chapter 7
Snowstorm

Several days passed. Bailey apologised and was kinder to her at school, but still the kids didn't seem to know how to treat her. *I'm just me!* she wanted to cry out to them – but at break time she couldn't go sliding or build snow forts with the others.

One day, Eldon's grandma came to talk to the class about making moccasins. As she set her supplies on Zoe's table, she gave her a warm smile. "So you're Eldon's new friend," she said. "This is the first time he's invited someone to go dog sledding."

Zoe felt her face go red. Ever since she'd made a fool of herself when the dog sled capsized, she'd been avoiding Eldon. It was embarrassing to know that she'd ruined the day for him. He'd probably decided that there was no point in being her friend. So it was best if she just stayed out of his way.

Around her, kids began whispering about dog sleds. Tyson and Eva gave her odd looks – but nobody laughed.

Zoe studied the unfinished moccasins on the table in front of her. The leather had an amazing sweet, smoky smell. Strips of fur looked so soft that her fingers crept out to touch them. A moccasin top sparkled with tiny beads sewn into a colourful flower.

The whispering stopped when Eldon's grandma started talking. Zoe listened, fascinated.

At break that day, she stayed inside. With Eldon's grandma's help, she stitched beads onto leather. It was complicated work, but she loved the feeling of the delicate little beads under her fingers. When the bell rang, the older woman smiled. "Take this home and finish it," she said to Zoe. "Then you can show me how it turns out."

Dad and Colin put up new walls in the dining room and the lobby. Zoe helped with the dusting before they painted.

When Bailey went up the ladder and had a conversation with the moose head as he dusted it, Zoe had to clutch her stomach because it was so funny. Just in time, she caught a photo of Bailey with Mum's camera. They'd been emailing photos home to Gram – including one of Zoe wheeling herself out to Colin's old van. The stray dog was in that photo, hanging around as usual. The scruffy dog was in the background, looking mean. Zoe was glad she hadn't noticed it at the time.

The stray husky was always there. Zoe dreaded going in or out of the inn. Every time, he trotted over, barking and wagging his tail. Sometimes, he propped his legs on the arm of her chair and tried to lick her face.

"He's *okay*, Zo!" Bailey said impatiently one day. "Can't you tell he likes you?"

Zoe shrank away from the whiskery muzzle with its cold, wet nose. "Go away," she said, and gave the dog a push. He obediently backed off, and then he lifted his leg.

"No!" Zoe yelled, waving her arms. "Get out of here!"

Bailey clapped his hand over his mouth, spluttering with laughter.

"Nikita!" Colin roared, getting out of a truck. "Mind your manners!"

With an embarrassed look, the dog slunk away from her.

Would Bailey torment her now about what had just happened? Zoe wheeled herself up the ramp and yanked the door open.

A snowstorm blew in that afternoon. Zoe sat at the window, staring at the swirling flakes. The house across the road became a ghost house, lost in whiteness. The wind gusted and howled like a banshee, rattling branches against the roof and flapping the plastic covering on the construction materials lying outside.

Gram phoned after supper. When it was Zoe's turn to talk, Gram went on and on about Zoe being safe. She hadn't liked the look of the dogs in the photo. She said they shouldn't be running loose, and that Zoe shouldn't be out in the snow alone. Halfway around the world, Gram sounded as strict as ever. Watching the blowing snow, Zoe wished it could blow into Gram's face.

Afterwards, Mum looked really cross. Soon, Zoe heard pots banging in the kitchen.

Zoe wheeled into the laundry room. As usual, heaps of dirty sheets and towels filled the baskets. Zoe grabbed a towel. Why did Gram have to be such an old grump? Mum worked hard all the time, and Gram had no right to make her unhappy. Frustrated, Zoe threw the towel. It hit a washing machine, then slid to the floor. She threw another towel. It plopped into the machine. Satisfied, Zoe grabbed a sheet.

It turned into a game. When she tried rebounding the towels and sheets off the ceiling, they swooshed as if they were alive. She wheeled as fast as she could to catch them. When a sheet draped all over her, she started laughing and couldn't stop. It was way better than hearing Gram's scolding.

When Mum helped Zoe into bed later, she wasn't cross any more. With the snow still blowing outside, Zoe felt satisfied and safe.

"What was all that noise in the laundry room?" Mum asked as she straightened up Zoe's covers.

Zoe giggled and then told Mum about the new game.

Mum laughed. "Gram means well. She worries about you a lot, sweetheart. But you're doing just fine, aren't you?" She bent to kiss Zoe's forehead. "Your beadwork is coming along nicely. Dad's enjoying it here . . . It's far more work than we ever imagined, but we can see the results."

Zoe snuggled into her warm bed. "Why is Bailey such a brat sometimes?" she asked.

"Give him a break, Zo," Mum replied. "It's not easy for him either, being here. Don't forget that he had to give up his place on the soccer team."

Yeah right, thought Zoe. Bailey had it so easy compared with her. Mum had no idea.

Chapter 8
Disaster!

At school, everybody was talking about a fishing derby that was coming up soon. Looking out the window at the blowing snow, Zoe couldn't imagine anybody sitting on the ice, fishing for two days. Especially herself.

"They build shacks and light bonfires on the ice," Tyson whispered loudly to Bailey. "We have hotdog roasts. The person who catches the biggest fish wins a bunch of money."

"Tyson." Mrs Piper's voice was stern. "What is Saskatchewan's third largest industry?"

Tyson's face was suddenly blank. Some of the girls giggled. Zoe almost did, too.

"Mining," Eldon said quietly.

Leah's hand was in the air. "Canada's the leading world producer of potash and uranium because of us," she said.

Zoe guessed Leah hadn't been listening either. She'd been doodling for the past while and was surprised to see that one of her doodles had turned into a husky. Her pencil made sharp ear tips on the doodle.

Was Eldon drawing anything? Zoe couldn't tell.

Bailey glanced her way. "Our dad said something about that," he said. "Before we came here."

Mrs Piper nodded. "Places like the North Star Inn are vital to our economy. Some of the miners come up here to work for long stretches and need a place to stay."

Zoe tried to draw the dog's nostrils. What did they look like? She ought to know – she'd seen enough dogs up close by now! She thought of Gram's phone call and how Gram was so worried about dogs running loose. But she was learning how to get around, and, if dogs could learn to pull a sled, they could learn that a wheelchair wasn't going to attack them. The big stray husky – Nik-something – knew how to keep out of her way.

Maybe those wild dogs really weren't so much of a problem. Besides, she was never out at night.

They had indoor gym because of the storm. Mrs Piper looked at Zoe. "Today we'll play basketball," she said.

Basketball! Now, that was something she *could* do!

At first, the other kids didn't know how to include her. Zoe could tell that they hadn't played much basketball. When Bailey got the ball and raced down the court with it, he passed to her instead of shooting. Surprised, Zoe eyed the hoop and made the shot. The ball swished through. To her astonishment, everybody cheered.

She looked over at Eldon. He was smiling at her, and her heart lifted. After that, she wheeled up and down the court with the others running beside her. By the end of the game, she'd made more baskets than Tyson.

After school the next day, Bailey was still excited about the fishing derby. "Mum!" he said when she arrived to pick them up. The other kids were all walking home, or sliding on the hill on the playground. "*Can* I go? Tyson says . . ."

Zoe stopped listening. Her face felt cold. So did her hands, in spite of her mittens. When the fishing derby came, what would *she* be doing? Watching TV at the North Star Inn?

"*Please*, Mum?" Bailey's voice broke into her thoughts. They were back at the inn.

Mum gave him a tired smile. "It sounds like fun," she said. "*Shoo!*" she added, yelling at the stray dog.

Zoe watched the dog slink away. His tail drooped. Usually it waved with happy wags.

"Coming, Zoe?" Mum called. "It's getting cold. Let's get inside."

As Zoe wheeled up the ramp, an icy patch sent her backwards. Setting the brakes, she stopped herself. Working at it, she got all the way up without help. After shedding her outdoor clothes, she took her homework to the TV room.

Mrs Piper had given them a big assignment, and she had a journal entry to write.

While her favourite afternoon shows flashed on the screen and the workers gradually returned from their jobs, she tackled the homework. Once it was finished, she opened her journal. Every day, they had to write about something that was on their minds. Mrs Piper always wrote encouraging notes at the bottom. Looking at the blank new page, Zoe tapped her pencil against the armrest of her chair.

Should she write about wondering if she'd be able to go to the fishing derby or about the dog-sledding incident?

As she sat there thinking, a heavy thud came from the kitchen. It was followed by an ear-piercing scream.

Mum! What had happened?

Dropping her books, Zoe raced down the hall as fast as she could.

It was like a nightmare, noisy and confusing. Men ran past her towards the kitchen. Zoe could hardly move. All she could see was people's backs and legs. She accidentally crashed into someone. "Mum!" she screamed.

Bailey appeared at her side. "What happened?" he asked.

"I don't know!"

Bailey squeezed through the crowd. When he finally got back, his face was white. "Mum's hurt," he choked. "She got burned cooking."

How could *Mum* get hurt? Suddenly, Zoe could hardly breathe. "Is it bad?"

Bailey nodded. "They're flying her out to a doctor."

Wasn't there a doctor in Uranium Point? Poor Mum! "I want to see her."

"It's too late," Bailey said. "They left already – Dad, too."

"*What*?" Zoe stared at him. "How could they leave us like that? Is Colin in charge?"

"Yeah, I guess."

What about all the getting-ready-for-bed things that Mum helped her with? And most important – would Mum be all right?

Construction workers and miners milled about in the hallway. Now there was a burning food smell. "I guess we should help," Zoe said. Her voice shook. 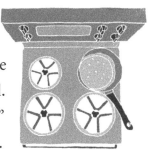 "Excuse me," she said, trying to get through.

The kitchen was a mess. Somebody was cleaning up a huge spill on the floor. On a back burner, a big pot sizzled ominously. Zoe couldn't reach the knob. "Bailey," she said, pointing. "Turn that off!"

Two cabbages sat on the counter. Mum had said something about coleslaw, and this was something she could do. Zoe rolled across the kitchen to get the butcher knife and the biggest cutting board. Balancing the board on her wheelchair arms, she started chopping.

Mum . . . hurt! Was she going to be okay? Would she have scars? How did she get burned? *Why did this have to happen?*

Chapter 9

Dog Alert

Zoe felt tears trickling down her cheeks. She kept on chopping. Now more people were in the kitchen – Eldon's mum from across the street and the woman who worked at the tiny gas station. A friendly hand patted her on the back. "You're a brave girl," someone said to her.

"Thanks," she whispered. It was so noisy. The loud fan was on, clearing the smoke from the charred pot. Zoe felt suffocated. She chopped harder.

The big knife slipped. Suddenly, a little piece of her fingernail lay there with the chopped cabbage. A tiny trickle of red spilled onto the cutting board.

Tears blinded her. Everything was too hard. She had to get out!

The entrance to the kitchen was blocked with people. Zoe put the cutting board on the counter. Nobody was near the back door. She wheeled herself over and let herself out.

The moon shone through the trees. It was freezing cold. Why hadn't she thought to bring her jacket? Zoe wiped her eyes. The quiet coldness cleared her thoughts. She'd get her jacket and then sit out the front. Anything was better than that noisy place where Mum . . . At the thought of Mum, tears slid down faster in cold streaks. She sniffled and wiped her eyes again, then reached up to let herself in.

The door was locked.

Zoe banged on the door. "Hey!" she shouted. "Let me in!" Somebody would be sure to notice.

Nobody came. She yelled and pounded some more. Did anybody know she was outside? Mum would've missed her. Dad, too. Was Bailey even there when she left?

Shivering, Zoe hugged herself. The moonlight showed a patch of smooth snow around the back of the North Star Inn.

Further from the building, the snow sloped downhill. She'd never been out here before.

There was only one thing to do. She'd push herself to the front entrance. If she got stuck, she'd yell and bang on somebody's window.

Determinedly, Zoe grabbed the rims of her wheels. The cold burned her hands and her fingers quickly went numb. It was hard to hold on.

"Help!" she yelled, near somebody's bedroom window.

In the distance, a dog barked.

In her mind's eye, she saw the sign at the airport. Panic screamed through her. She took a breath of freezing air and tried to calm herself. People were nearby. She'd be safe.

The surface of the snow looked smooth, but underneath it was bumpy. Zoe felt the front wheels hit one buried obstacle after another. At her next hard tug at the wheels, her chair tilted.

Dog Alert

Before Zoe could figure out what was happening, her wheelchair was sliding, rolling, tumbling downhill. *Killer Hill!* Numbly, she remembered Bailey talking about it, and how the North Star Inn was on one of the slopes. Branches whipped her face as her runaway chair crashed into a tree, then kept going.

When her chair finally stopped, it was upside-down in the snow. Snow filled her mouth and plugged her nose. She spat it out. It was darker here under the trees and she couldn't see much.

"Mum!" Zoe yelled, even though she knew her mother was nowhere near. "*Mum!*" Fumbling with the frigid buckle, she finally freed herself from her upside-down chair and fell into a shivering heap.

There was a floundering sound in the snow. Somebody was coming.

Relieved, Zoe pushed her head and shoulders up. "Bailey?" she called.

Whatever it was, it wasn't Bailey. A dark form appeared – no, it was several of them. Feet padded. Breath snuffled.

As her eyes adjusted to the dark, Zoe made out the shape of not one but several dogs. And they were surrounding her.

Her heart slammed in her chest.

Maybe it was the husky, Nik-whatever, and Sparkles and some of the other dogs that were always around. "Sparkles?" she said, hopefully. "Niki?" Her voice didn't work properly.

But no dog came to lick her face. Bad breath hung around her in a cloud. The dogs started circling. Then the snarling began. Zoe saw sharp teeth glinting in the darkness.

She screamed – but who would hear her out here?

The dogs' movements quickened and they pressed in closer.

Maybe if she played dead, it would fool them and they'd go away.

She tried to make herself go limp. It didn't work. Her teeth were chattering like little hammers. The dogs weren't fooled. One darted towards her hand, but another pushed it away. *Blood* . . . Zoe remembered the finger she'd cut with the butcher knife. She tried to yell. All that came out was a squeak.

The space around her was electric with dogs pacing, snarling and snapping . . . How long would it take before one of them attacked her? Could she possibly grab her wheelchair, maybe yank it over her? She could hear herself gasping.

Suddenly, an unearthly howl made her quiver all over, inside and out.

"Zoe!"

She pushed up at the far-off sound of voices calling. "I'm here!" she screamed, but her throat was dry. She yelled again and again. The dogs paced around her.

As the voices died out, the dog nearest her stiffened. It growled, deep in its throat.

This had to be a bad dream. Why couldn't she wake up?

Then she heard distant barking growing louder. Were more dogs coming? She felt hot tears wet her cheeks as she buried her head in the snow.

The darkness exploded into a savage fury of growling and snapping. She waited for the pain of the first bite, but none came. Seconds passed.

Slowly, she looked up – and couldn't believe her eyes. There, among the growling mass, was a dog she recognised instantly – Nikita! The snarling dogs had turned their attention away from Zoe and were now focused on the husky.

Zoe seized the chance and grabbed the frame of her wheelchair, yanking it hard. At first, the chair wouldn't move – it was sunk into the snow. But, with another hard tug, it slid towards her and then, finally, over the top half of her body.

She screamed as loudly as she could.

Now voices were yelling again. Torch beams darted across the snow. There was a loud gunshot.

Then, the sound of dogs running through heavy snow. Finally, it was quiet, except for people calling her name . . . and a dog whimpering beside her.

Chapter 10
Nikita

Everything blurred. She was being carried. Then she was inside, wrapped in sleeping bags. Bailey stared down at her. People hovered, checking her hands, her feet. "Her poor, cold feet!" somebody said. She must have dozed off, because now there was a sweet, smoky smell. Eldon's grandma was adjusting her legs. Zoe caught a glimpse of furry moccasins on her feet.

Later, when she opened her eyes, she was in her own bed. Mrs Piper was there. "It's good to see you awake, Zoe," her teacher said. "I'll stay with you and Bailey tonight. Your dad phoned a little while ago. Your mother is going to be all right. They'll be flying back home tomorrow."

A great wave of relief washed through her. Before she could drift off again, Bailey sat on her bed. "That dog!" he said. "Nikita. He saved your life, Zo."

"Is he okay?" her voice rasped.

"He's got bites all over. Those wild dogs – he's got a bloody ear and . . ."

Mrs Piper's hand was on Bailey's shoulder. "Nikita is pretty sore right now, but he'll be fine." She smiled. "You have a true friend, Zoe."

Suddenly, Zoe's eyes felt watery. She thought of all the times she'd yelled at the dog. "Can I see him?" she asked.

Mrs Piper pondered for a moment. "Usually, dogs stay outside. With their thick fur, they get too hot indoors."

"I'll get him!" Bailey hurried out.

Zoe looked up at her teacher. Feelings choked her throat, things she couldn't figure out how to say.

Mrs Piper understood. She patted Zoe's shoulder. "In Uranium Point, we look out for our neighbours. We may be so tiny and remote that we're not on most of the maps, but the people here are the best."

When Bailey returned with Nikita, the big stray limped straight to Zoe's bed. One of his ears was bitten and bloody. He thrust his face towards her.

Zoe rolled herself sideways and reached out to him. As she stroked his soft, furry head and neck, a warm wet tongue kissed her cheeks. Then, stiffly, the dog settled himself on the floor. He sighed and fell asleep.

Mum and Dad got back the next morning. Although it was a school day, Zoe and Bailey stayed home to wait for them. Mum's arm was bandaged, and she was pale and weak. After hugs and listening with horror to Zoe's adventure of the night before, Mum had to go and lie down.

Dad sat with Zoe in the TV room. When he put his arm around her, Zoe could feel him shaking. "I'm so sorry!" he said.

His voice was shaking, too. "I never should've left you like that. We had no idea . . ."

Zoe swallowed hard. Mum and Dad hadn't actually been gone very long, but to think what happened while they were away! She couldn't forgive Dad – not yet, anyhow. "It was scary," she said at last.

Dad sighed. "Your mum and I are thinking about telling Colin this job is more than we can handle. We had no idea coming here would put your life at risk."

Zoe looked down because Dad's eyes were too sad. Probably Gram *had* been right. Zoe shuddered as she thought about what the wild dogs might have done to her . . . or how she could've frozen to death.

On TV, a show for little kids was playing. Its colourful characters and happy music made her want to be with kids her own age, not with Mum and Dad, who were feeling so guilty.

"I'm going to school," she said.

Dad was taken aback. "I suppose I could drive you. I was kind of hoping . . ."

Anger flashed through her. "I'll take myself."

Dad's mouth hung open. "Bailey?" he called. "Could you . . ."

"I said, *I'll take myself*!" Zoe said as she wheeled out of the TV room. She grabbed her jacket off the hook on the wall and pulled it on. She looked down at her feet. She was still wearing the moccasins that Eldon's grandma had given her. It would be too hard to get her boots on – but the moccasins would be fine. After all, she wouldn't be walking through the snow.

Nikita was waiting outside.

Tears rose in her eyes. "Oh, Nikita. *Thank you*!" She leaned towards him. The dog snuffled in her ear, then licked her face. Zoe held still, letting him lick. "I'm so sorry I yelled at you all those times," she whispered.

"Zoe?" Dad called. "Wait. I wish you wouldn't . . ."

Suddenly, she needed to punish Dad, who'd left without telling her. Yes, it was an emergency, but still he should've told her and Bailey. She turned and wheeled down the new ramp. Although Dad followed, she didn't look back.

The hilly road would be tricky with its snow and ice, but *nothing* could be as bad as what happened last night. And Nikita was staying by her side. This time, the big husky made her feel safe. By carefully setting and releasing her brakes, she managed to keep her chair under control on the hilly spots.

When she arrived at school, she was hot and sweaty, despite the cold. At the same time, she had a great feeling of accomplishment. Mum and Dad would be proud of her – and Gram would be shocked.

Nikita grinned at her. Then he trotted across the playground and disappeared into a patch of trees.

The secretary held the front door open. "Welcome, Zoe!" she said.

Zoe sat up straighter. "How'd you know I was coming?"

The secretary winked. "Your dad needs to know you arrived safely. Where's your brother?"

"Bailey?" She improvised quickly. "He's got a sore throat."

When she rolled into the classroom, everybody let out a cheer. Eldon raced over and gave her a high five. The kids were so full of questions that Mrs Piper didn't even try to keep order for a while.

When the class still didn't settle down, Mrs Piper blinked the lights off and on. "Okay," she said. "We'll take our gym period now." She turned to Zoe. "Zoe, what shall we do for gym? It can be an outdoor or indoor activity."

Zoe looked at her new teacher, who was so kind, and at her new friends. Eldon seemed worried. Eva smiled at her. Even Tyson looked at her with respect.

"Can we go sliding, please?" she asked.

The class went quiet. Here and there, Zoe heard confused murmurs. "I have an idea," she said, and explained.

Outside, Nikita came to check on her. Nobody shooed him away. The sun was brilliant on the snow. Birds sang in the trees – chickadees, Mrs Piper said.

Kids crowded around to assist Zoe out of her wheelchair. She reached for Eldon's shoulders and leaned on him as everybody helped her onto Tyson's red slider. Mrs Piper fastened a strap across Zoe's legs to hold them in place.

What had Dad said about going home early? Zoe knew suddenly that she wanted to stay in Uranium Point as long as possible.

Dog Alert

She'd gone dog sledding. She'd survived tumbling downhill at night, and she'd escaped from a pack of wild dogs. Now she was doing this. The fishing derby was coming up, and she couldn't miss that!

Eldon and Tyson pulled her up the playground hill. Zoe could hear them puffing. Nikita trotted beside her. Everyone's breath trailed clouds. At the top of the hill, she looked down the slope, and took a deep breath. "Ready!" she said.

Friendly hands gave her a push. Then Zoe went flying downhill. She couldn't stop laughing.